Cool Sports Facts

Cool Skateboarding Facts

by Sandy Donovan

Consulting Editor: Gail Saunders-Smith, PhD

Consultants: Mimi Knoop and Drew Mearns
Founders, Action Sports Alliance, Inc.
and Anti-Gravity Skatepark & Skateshop

CAPSTONE PRESS
a capstone imprint

Pebble Plus is published by Capstone Press,
151 Good Counsel Drive, P.O. Box 669, Mankato, Minnesota 56002.
www.capstonepub.com

Books published by Capstone Press are manufactured with paper containing at least 10 percent post-consumer waste.

Library of Congress Cataloging-in-Publication Data
Donovan, Sandra, 1967–
  Cool skateboarding facts / by Sandy Donovan.
    p. cm. — (Pebble plus. Cool sports facts)
  Includes bibliographical references and index.
  Summary: "Simple text and full-color photos illustrate facts about the history, equipment, tricks, and records of skateboarding"—Provided by publisher.
  ISBN 978-1-4296-5303-9 (library binding)
  ISBN 978-1-4296-6203-1 (paperback)
  1. Skateboarding—Juvenile literature. I. Title. II. Series.
GV859.8.D66 2011
796.22—dc22   2010028901

Editorial Credits
Katy Kudela, editor; Kyle Grenz, designer; Eric Gohl, media researcher; Laura Manthe, production specialist

Photo Credits
Alamy/Ultimate Group, LLC, 13
Capstone Studio/Karon Dubke, 11
Corbis/Bettmann, 7; NewSport/Steve Boyle, 19; NewSport/X Games IX/Matt A. Brown, 17
Getty Images Inc./Cameron Spencer, cover; Focus on Sport, 9
Newscom/Icon SMI/Imaginechina/Hu Jinxi, 21
Shutterstock/Galina Barskaya, 5; mimon!, 4, 14, 20; Shmel, cover (skateboard), back cover, 1; Troy Kellogg, 15

Note to Parents and Teachers

The Cool Sports Facts series supports national social studies standards related to people, places, and culture. This book describes and illustrates skateboarding. The images support early readers in understanding the text. The repetition of words and phrases helps early readers learn new words. This book also introduces early readers to subject-specific vocabulary words, which are defined in the Glossary section. Early readers may need assistance to read some words and to use the Table of Contents, Glossary, Read More, Internet Sites, and Index sections of the book.

Printed in the United States of America in North Mankato, Minnesota.

092010   005933CGS11

Table of Contents

Shred It Up

About 13 million people ride
skateboards in the United States.
They ride on streets or go to
one of 2,000 skate parks.

Cool History

The first skateboarders were California surfers. For fun, they attached wooden boards to roller skate wheels.

By the 1960s people were buying skateboards.

7

The first skaters found unusual places to skate. Many used empty swimming pools. The idea caught on. People built skate parks with pools.

Cool Equipment

Skateboards are not all alike.

Smaller boards give

street skaters control.

Longboards give skaters

speed going down big hills.

11

On a half-pipe, skaters catch air!
They boost off the ramp's lip.
They do twists and other tricks
while in the air.

Cool Tricks

Most skaters first learn to ollie.

Skaters ollie when they jump

with their board.

They don't use their hands.

Tony Hawk developed

more than 100 tricks.

For the trick called the 900,

he makes two and a half turns

in the air.

Cool Records

Lauren Perkins won first place

at the 2000 Gravity Games

amateur contest.

Her amazing tricks

beat out 45 boys.

Lauren Perkins at the 2004 Gravity Games.

In 2005 Danny Way set

a world record.

He jumped over the

Great Wall of China.

And he did this jump five times!

Glossary

amateur—someone who takes part in a sport without being paid

boost—to raise or lift by pushing up from below

catch air—the time spent in the air between a jump's takeoff and landing

Gravity Games—a competition for extreme sports, such as skateboarding, snowboarding, in-line skating, and BMX

half-pipe—a U-shaped ramp with high walls

900—two and a half rotations done during an air trick

ollie—a jump into the air without using hands to hold onto the board

Read More

DeGezelle, Terri. *Let's Skateboard!* Sports and Activities. Mankato, Minn.: Capstone Press, 2006.

Mahaney, Ian F. *Tony Hawk: Skateboarding Champion.* Extreme Sports Biographies. New York: Rosen Pub. Group, 2005.

Internet Sites

FactHound offers a safe, fun way to find Internet sites related to this book. All of the sites on FactHound have been researched by our staff.

Here's all you do:

Visit *www.facthound.com*

Type in this code: 9781429653039

Index

Word Count: 186

Grade: 1

Early-Intervention Level: 20